WORD MASTERY

Step-by-Step Exercises & Tasks

By

RAHIM DEEDS

Table of Contents

Introduction:

Welcome to "Word Mastery : Step By Step Exercises & Tasks." As the author of this book, I am delighted to embark on this journey of exploring the vast potential of Microsoft Word and unlocking your creative prowess.

In today's digital age, Microsoft Word has become an indispensable tool for professionals, students, writers, and designers alike. It is a versatile platform that goes beyond traditional word processing, offering a wide array of features and functionalities that can transform your ideas into visually stunning and impactful creations.

In this comprehensive guide, we will delve into the depths of Microsoft Word, unraveling its hidden gems and empowering you to take full advantage of its capabilities. Whether you are a novice seeking to enhance your document formatting skills or an experienced user looking to push the boundaries of your creative expression, this book is designed to meet your needs.

Throughout the chapters, you will find step-by-step instructions, practical exercises, and insider tips to help you navigate the software with ease. We will cover everything from formatting texts with precision to designing compelling graphics, creating captivating presentations, and exploring advanced features that will set your work apart.

But this book is not just about mastering a software tool; it is about tapping into your innate creativity and unleashing your imagination. As we progress, I will share insights, inspiration, and techniques to nurture your creative spark and infuse it into every document you create.

I invite you to embark on this exciting journey with me. Together, we will unlock the full potential of Microsoft Word and empower you to create remarkable, professional-grade documents that make an impact. Whether you are a student, professional, writer, or aspiring designer, this book will serve as your trusted companion; guiding you through the intricacies of Word and helping you discover new dimensions of creativity.

Get ready to embark on an adventure that will transform the way you approach document creation and unleash the artist within you. Let's dive in and begin our exploration of "Word Mastery : Step By Step Exercises & Tasks."

Happy creating!

Rahim deeds

Author of "Word Mastery : Step By Step Exercises & Tasks"

Exercise:
Creating A Simple Document

Step 1: Open Microsoft Word

Click on the Microsoft Word icon on your desktop or search for it in your Windows search bar.

Step 2: Create a new document

Once you have opened Microsoft Word, select "Blank Document" from the menu or click on "New Document."

Step 3: Enter text

In the new document, type the following text:

Hello, World! This is my first document.

Step 4: Format text

Highlight the text "Hello, World!" and click on the "Bold" button in the toolbar. Then, highlight "This is my first document" and click on the "Italic" button in the toolbar.

Step 5: Add a heading

Click anywhere above the text and type "My First Document" to create a heading. Highlight the heading and select "Heading 1" from the Styles drop-down menu.

Step 6: Save the document

Click on "File" and then "Save As" to save the document. Choose a file name and select the location where you want to save the file. Click on "Save."

Step 7: Close the document

Click on "File" and then "Close" to close the document.

Exercise:
Practical Step By Step Font Group

1. Open Microsoft Word and create a new document.

2. Type the following sentence: "The quick brown fox jumps over the lazy dog."

3. Change the font of the sentence to Arial.

4. Change the font size of the sentence to 16.

5. Change the font color of the sentence to red.

6. Underline the word "lazy".

7. Italicize the word "fox".

8. Bold the word "jumps".

9. Strike through the word "brown".

10. Type the following sentence: "H2O is a chemical formula for water."

11. Make the "2" in H2O a subscript.

12. Make the "O" in H2O a superscript.

13. Highlight the word "chemical".

14. Change the case of the sentence to all uppercase.

15. Save the document as "Font Formatting Exercise".

Exercise:
Exploring More Fonts In Microsoft Word

Step 1: Open Microsoft Word

Click on the Microsoft Word icon on your desktop or search for it in your Windows search bar.

Step 2: Create a new document

Once you have opened Microsoft Word, select "Blank Document" from the menu or click on "New Document."

Step 3: Type some text

Type the following sentence into the document:

"Learning about fonts is fun!"

Step 4: Change the font style

Highlight the text "Learning about fonts" in the sentence you typed. Then, click on the "Font" drop-down menu in the toolbar. Explore the different font options available, such as Arial, Times New Roman, Calibri, etc. Select a different font style of your choice.

Step 5: Change the font size

Now, select the entire sentence "Learning about fonts is fun!" by clicking and dragging the cursor across the text. Click on the "Font Size" drop-down menu in the toolbar. Try different font sizes, such as 12pt, 16pt, or 20pt. Choose a font size that you prefer.

Step 6: Change the font color

With the entire sentence still selected, click on the "Font Color" button in the toolbar. A color palette will appear. Experiment with different colors by selecting them. Choose a color that stands out and suits your preference.

Step 7: Apply text effects

Highlight the word "fun!" in the sentence. Click on the "Bold" button in the toolbar to make the word bold. Then, click on the "Italic" button to make the word italicized. Observe how the text changes in appearance.

Step 8: Save the document

Click on "File" and then "Save As" to save the document. Choose a file name and select the location where you want to save the file. Click on "Save."

Step 9: Close the document

Click on "File" and then "Close" to close the document.

Exercise:
Formatting Text In Microsoft Word

Step 1: Open Microsoft Word

Click on the Microsoft Word icon on your desktop or search for it in your Windows search bar.

Step 2: Create a new document

Once you have opened Microsoft Word, select "Blank Document" from the menu or click on "New Document."

Step 3: Type some text

Type the following sentence into the document:

"I love using Microsoft Word for my documents."

Step 4: Apply underline formatting

Highlight the word "using" in the sentence you typed. Then, click on the "Underline" button in the toolbar to apply underline formatting to the word.

Step 5: Apply bold formatting

Now, select the word "Microsoft" in the sentence. Click on the "Bold" button in the toolbar to make the word bold.

Step 6: Apply italic formatting

With the entire sentence still selected, click on the "Italic" button in the toolbar to make the entire sentence italicized.

Step 7: Change the case of text

Highlight the word "Word" in the sentence. Click on the "Change Case" button in the toolbar. In the drop-down menu, select "UPPERCASE" to change the word to uppercase.

Step 8: Save the document

Click on "File" and then "Save As" to save the document. Choose a
file name and select the location where you want to save the file. Click
on "Save."

Step 9: Close the document

Click on "File" and then "Close" to close the document.

Exercise:
Advanced Text Formatting In Microsoft Word

Step 1: Open Microsoft Word

Click on the Microsoft Word icon on your desktop or search for it in your Windows search bar.

Step 2: Create a new document

Once you have opened Microsoft Word, select "Blank Document" from the menu or click on "New Document."

Step 3: Type some text

Type the following sentence into the document:

"I enjoy learning new features in Microsoft Word."

Step 4: Apply strikethrough formatting

Highlight the word "enjoy" in the sentence you typed. Then, click on the "Strikethrough" button in the toolbar to apply strikethrough formatting to the word.

Step 5: Apply subscript formatting

Now, select the number "2" in the sentence. Right-click on the selected number and choose "Font" from the context menu. In the Font dialog box, check the "Subscript" option and click "OK" to apply subscript formatting to the number.

Step 6: Apply superscript formatting

With the entire sentence still selected, right-click on the selected text and choose "Font" from the context menu. In the Font dialog box, check the "Superscript" option and click "OK" to apply superscript formatting to the sentence.

Step 7: Save the document

Click on "File" and then "Save As" to save the document. Choose a file name and select the location where you want to save the file. Click on "Save."

Step 8: Close the document

Click on "File" and then "Close" to close the document.

Exercise:
Using Bullets And Numbers In Microsoft Word

Step 1: Open Microsoft Word

Click on the Microsoft Word icon on your desktop or search for it in your Windows search bar.

Step 2: Create a new document

Once you have opened Microsoft Word, select "Blank Document" from the menu or click on "New Document."

Step 3: Type a list of items

Type the following list of items into the document:

Apples

Bananas

Oranges

Grapes

Step 4: Apply bullet points

With the entire list selected, click on the "Bullets" button in the toolbar. The list items should now be formatted with bullet points.

Step 5: Create a numbered list

Press "Enter" on your keyboard to create a new line. Type the following sentence:

"I bought 5 apples, 3 bananas, and 2 oranges."

Step 6: Apply numbering

Highlight the sentence you typed in Step 5. Click on the "Numbering" button in the toolbar. The sentence should now be formatted as a numbered list.

Step 7: Indent sub-items

Press "Enter" on your keyboard to create a new line below the "Apples" item. Type "Red Delicious" and press "Enter" again. Type "Granny Smith." Highlight both sub-items ("Red Delicious" and "Granny Smith") and click on the "Increase Indent" button in the toolbar. Notice how the sub-items are now indented under the "Apples" bullet point.

Step 8: Save the document

Click on "File" and then "Save As" to save the document. Choose a file name and select the location where you want to save the file. Click on "Save."

Step 9: Close the document

Click on "File" and then "Close" to close the document.

Exercise Title:
Formatting A Document With Bullets, Numbering, Indents, Alignments, Lines, And Paragraphs

Instructions:

1. Open a new blank document in Microsoft Word.
2. Type the following text into the document:

   <u>**Top Ten Places to Visit**</u>
   <u>Paris, France</u>
   <u>Tokyo, Japan</u>
   <u>New York City, USA</u>
   <u>Rome, Italy</u>
   <u>Sydney, Australia</u>
   <u>Barcelona, Spain</u>
   <u>Dubai, UAE</u>
   <u>Rio de Janeiro, Brazil</u>
   <u>Bangkok, Thailand</u>
   <u>Vancouver, Canada</u>

3. Apply bullets to the list of top ten places to visit. You can choose any bullet style you like.
4. Apply numbering to the list of top ten places to visit (retype the list in number 2).
5. Indent the list of top ten places to visit so that it is aligned with the rest of the text in the document.
6. Align the list of top ten places to visit to the left side of the page.
7. Add a horizontal line below the list of top ten places to visit.
8. Add a paragraph of text below the horizontal line. The paragraph can be about any topic you choose.
9. Format the paragraph with a hanging indent.
10. Add a bullet list within the paragraph you just created. The list should contain at least three items.

11. Align the bullet list within the paragraph to the left side of the page.
12. Add a numbered list within the paragraph you just created. The list should contain at least three items.
13. Format the numbered list with a right indent.
14. Save the document.

Exercise:
Applying Text Highlight, Font Color, And Shading In Microsoft Word

Step 1: Open Microsoft Word

Click on the Microsoft Word icon on your desktop or search for it in your Windows search bar.

Step 2: Create a new document

Once you have opened Microsoft Word, select "Blank Document" from the menu or click on "New Document."

Step 3: Type some text

Type the following sentence into the document:

"I like to highlight important information in my documents."

Step 4: Apply text highlight

Highlight the word "highlight" in the sentence you typed. Then, click on the "Text Highlight Color" button in the toolbar. Choose a color from the color palette to apply as a highlight to the selected text.

Step 5: Apply font color

With the entire sentence still selected, click on the "Font Color" button in the toolbar. Choose a different color from the color palette to change the color of the text in the sentence.

Step 6: Apply shading to a paragraph

Press "Enter" on your keyboard to create a new paragraph below the sentence you typed. Type the following sentence:

"This paragraph will have a shaded background."

Highlight the entire paragraph you just typed. Click on the "Shading" button in the toolbar. Choose a color from the color palette to apply as a background shading to the selected paragraph.

Step 7: Save the document

Click on "File" and then "Save As" to save the document. Choose a file name and select the location where you want to save the file. Click on "Save."

Step 8: Close the document

Click on "File" and then "Close" to close the document.

Exercise:
Indenting, Aligning, And Adjusting Line Spacing In Microsoft Word

Step 1: Open Microsoft Word

Click on the Microsoft Word icon on your desktop or search for it in your Windows search bar.

Step 2: Create a new document

Once you have opened Microsoft Word, select "Blank Document" from the menu or click on "New Document."

Step 3: Type some text

Type the following paragraph into the document:

"Lorem ipsum dolor sit amet, consecteturadipiscingelit. Phasellus vitae velitutestplaceratfringilla. Sed gravida, nequenec tempus iaculis, lorem nequealiquetodio, in ullamcorper lorem sapien vitae elit."

Step 4: Indent the paragraph

Click anywhere in the paragraph you typed. Then, click on the "Increase Indent" button in the toolbar. Notice how the entire paragraph is indented to the right.

Step 5: Align the paragraph

With the paragraph still selected, click on the "Align Left" button in the toolbar to align the paragraph to the left margin. Observe how the paragraph adjusts its position.

Step 6: Adjust line spacing

Highlight the entire paragraph. Click on the "Line Spacing" button in the toolbar. From the drop-down menu, select "1.5" to adjust the line spacing to 1.5 times the normal spacing.

Step 7: Save the document

Click on "File" and then "Save As" to save the document. Choose a file name and select the location where you want to save the file. Click on "Save."

Step 8: Close the document

Click on "File" and then "Close" to close the document.

Exercise:
Applying Letter Styles In Microsoft Word

Step 1: Open Microsoft Word

Click on the Microsoft Word icon on your desktop or search for it in your Windows search bar.

Step 2: Create a new document

Once you have opened Microsoft Word, select "Blank Document" from the menu or click on "New Document."

Step 3: Type a letter heading

Type the following text at the top of the document:

Your Name

Your Address

City, State, ZIP Code

Date

Step 4: Apply a letterhead style

Highlight the entire letter heading you typed in Step 3. Click on the "Styles" drop-down menu in the toolbar. From the list of styles, select "Heading 1" or any other predefined letterhead style to apply it to the heading. Observe how the heading changes in appearance.

Step 5: Type the recipient's address

Press "Enter" on your keyboard to create a new line below the date. Type the recipient's name and address, aligning it to the left margin. For example:

Recipient's Name

Recipient's Address

City, State, ZIP Code

Step 6: Apply a recipient address style

Highlight the entire recipient's address you typed in Step 5. Click on the "Styles" drop-down menu in the toolbar. Select a predefined recipient address style from the list of styles to apply it. Notice how the recipient's address changes in appearance.

Step 7: Type the letter content

Press "Enter" on your keyboard to create a new line below the recipient's address. Type the content of the letter, addressing the recipient. For example:

Dear [Recipient's Name],

I hope this letter finds you well. ...

Step 8: Apply a letter body style

Highlight the entire content of the letter you typed in Step 7. Click on the "Styles" drop-down menu in the toolbar. Choose a predefined letter body style from the list of styles to apply it. Observe how the letter content changes in appearance.

Step 9: Save the document

Click on "File" and then "Save As" to save the document. Choose a file name and select the location where you want to save the file. Click on "Save."

Step 10: Close the document

Click on "File" and then "Close" to close the document.

Exercise:
Applying "AA" Style In Microsoft Word

Step 1: Open Microsoft Word

Click on the Microsoft Word icon on your desktop or search for it in your Windows search bar.

Step 2: Create a new document

Once you have opened Microsoft Word, select "Blank Document" from the menu or click on "New Document."

Step 3: Type a paragraph of text

Type the following paragraph into the document:

Lorem ipsum dolor sit amet, consecteturadipiscingelit. Phasellus vitae velitutestplaceratfringilla. Sed gravida, nequenec tempus iaculis, lorem nequealiquetodio, in ullamcorper lorem sapien vitae elit.

Step 4: Select the entire paragraph

Click and drag your mouse cursor to select the entire paragraph you typed in Step 3. Alternatively, you can place your cursor at the beginning of the paragraph, hold the Shift key, and press the Down Arrow key until the whole paragraph is selected.

Step 5: Apply "AA" style

In the toolbar, locate the "Styles" drop-down menu. Click on it and scroll down to find the "AA" style. Click on the "AA" style to apply it to the selected paragraph. Observe how the paragraph's appearance changes according to the "AA" style.

Step 6: Save the document

Click on "File" and then "Save As" to save the document. Choose a file name and select the location where you want to save the file. Click on "Save."

Step 7: Close the document

Click on "File" and then "Close" to close the document.

Exercise:
Using The "Find" And "Replace" Functions In Microsoft Word

Step 1: Open Microsoft Word

Click on the Microsoft Word icon on your desktop or search for it in your Windows search bar.

Step 2: Create a new document

Once you have opened Microsoft Word, select "Blank Document" from the menu or click on "New Document."

Step 3: Type some text

Type the following sentence multiple times in the document:

"The quick brown fox jumps over the lazy dog."

Step 4: Find a word

Click on the "Home" tab in the toolbar. Locate the "Find" button or press the "Ctrl" + "F" keyboard shortcut. In the "Find" dialog box that appears, type the word "fox" and click "Find Next." Observe how Microsoft Word finds and highlights the first occurrence of the word "fox" in the document.

Step 5: Replace a word

In the "Find" dialog box, click on the "Replace" tab. In the "Find what" field, type the word "fox." In the "Replace with" field, type the word "cat." Click on "Replace" to replace the currently selected occurrence of the word "fox" with the word "cat." Repeat this step to replace additional occurrences of the word "fox" with "cat" as desired.

Step 6: Replace all occurrences

Still in the "Replace" tab of the "Find" dialog box, click on "Replace All" to replace all remaining occurrences of the word "fox" with the word "cat" in the entire document. Observe how Microsoft Word replaces all instances of the word "fox" with "cat" automatically.

Step 7: Save the document

Click on "File" and then "Save As" to save the document. Choose a file name and select the location where you want to save the file. Click on "Save."

Step 8: Close the document

Click on "File" and then "Close" to close the document.

Exercise:
Creating A Table In Microsoft Word

Step 1: Open Microsoft Word

Click on the Microsoft Word icon on your desktop or search for it in your Windows search bar.

Step 2: Create a new document

Once you have opened Microsoft Word, select "Blank Document" from the menu or click on "New Document."

Step 3: Insert a table

Click on the "Insert" tab in the toolbar. In the "Tables" section, click on the "Table" button. A grid will appear.

Step 4: Specify the table size

Hover your mouse over the grid to specify the number of rows and columns for your table. Left-click to create a 3x3 table (3 rows and 3 columns).

Step 5: Enter content into the table

Type the following content into the table:

Fruit	Quantity	Color
Apple	2	Red
Orange	3	Orange
Banana	4	Yellow

Step 6: Customize the table

With the table selected, you can customize its appearance using the options available in the "Table Design" or "Table Layout" tabs in the toolbar. For example, you can change the table style, adjust cell width and height, merge cells, and more.

Step 7: Save the document

Click on "File" and then "Save As" to save the document. Choose a file name and select the location where you want to save the file. Click on "Save."

Step 8: Close the document

Click on "File" and then "Close" to close the document.

Exercise:
Inserting A Picture In Microsoft Word

Step 1: Open Microsoft Word

Click on the Microsoft Word icon on your desktop or search for it in your Windows search bar.

Step 2: Create a new document

Once you have opened Microsoft Word, select "Blank Document" from the menu or click on "New Document."

Step 3: Position the cursor

Click on the location in the document where you want to insert the picture.

Step 4: Insert the picture

Click on the "Insert" tab in the toolbar. In the "Illustrations" section, click on the "Picture" button. A file dialog box will open.

Step 5: Select the picture file

Browse your computer to find the picture file you want to insert. Select the file and click on the "Insert" button. The picture will be inserted into the document at the cursor's location.

Step 6: Resize and position the picture

Click and drag the corners of the picture to resize it, if needed. You can also click and drag the picture to reposition it within the document.

Step 7: Adjust picture settings (optional)

With the picture selected, you can access additional options and settings in the "Picture Format" tab in the toolbar. Here, you can adjust the picture's brightness, contrast, and other image properties.

Step 8: Save the document

Click on "File" and then "Save As" to save the document. Choose a file name and select the location where you want to save the file. Click on "Save."

Step 9: Close the document

Click on "File" and then "Close" to close the document.

Exercise:
Adding Shapes And Smartart
In Microsoft Word

Step 1: Open Microsoft Word

Click on the Microsoft Word icon on your desktop or search for it in your Windows search bar.

Step 2: Create a new document

Once you have opened Microsoft Word, select "Blank Document" from the menu or click on "New Document."

Step 3: Insert a shape

Click on the "Insert" tab in the toolbar. In the "Illustrations" section, click on the "Shapes" button. A drop-down menu with various shapes will appear.

Step 4: Select a shape

Choose a shape from the menu, such as a rectangle or a circle. Click and drag on the document to draw the shape. Release the mouse button when you are satisfied with the size of the shape.

Step 5: Customize the shape

With the shape selected, you can customize its appearance using the options available in the "Shape Format" tab in the toolbar. For example, you can change the fill color, outline color, add effects, and more.

Step 6: Insert SmartArt

Click on the "Insert" tab in the toolbar. In the "Illustrations" section, click on the "SmartArt" button. A gallery of SmartArt graphics will appear.

Step 7: Choose a SmartArt graphic

Select a SmartArt graphic that suits your needs, such as a process diagram or a hierarchy. Click on the chosen graphic to insert it into the document.

Step 8: Edit the SmartArt graphic

With the SmartArt graphic selected, you can enter text into the provided placeholders. Simply click on a placeholder and start typing. You can also add or remove shapes, change the layout, and modify the appearance using the options in the "SmartArt Design" or "SmartArt Format" tabs in the toolbar.

Step 9: Save the document

Click on "File" and then "Save As" to save the document. Choose a file name and select the location where you want to save the file. Click on "Save."

Step 10: Close the document

Click on "File" and then "Close" to close the document.

Exercise:
Creating A Chart In Microsoft Word

Step 1: Open Microsoft Word

Click on the Microsoft Word icon on your desktop or search for it in your Windows search bar.

Step 2: Create a new document

Once you have opened Microsoft Word, select "Blank Document" from the menu or click on "New Document."

Step 3: Insert a chart

Click on the "Insert" tab in the toolbar. In the "Illustrations" section, click on the "Chart" button. A dialog box will appear with various chart types to choose from.

Step 4: Select a chart type

Choose a chart type that suits your needs, such as a column chart or a pie chart. Select the desired chart type and click on the "OK" button. A sample chart will be inserted into the document.

Step 5: Enter data for the chart

In the Excel spreadsheet that appears, enter your own data for the chart. You can replace the sample data with your own values or copy and paste data from another source. Make sure to include appropriate labels for the data series and categories.

Step 6: Customize the chart

With the chart selected, you can customize its appearance and formatting using the options available in the "Chart Design" and "Chart Format" tabs in the toolbar. You can change the chart style, add titles, adjust axis labels, and more.

Step 7: Save the document

Click on "File" and then "Save As" to save the document. Choose a file name and select the location where you want to save the file. Click on "Save."

Step 8: Close the document

Click on "File" and then "Close" to close the document.

Exercise:
Adding Header, Footer, And Page Numbers In Microsoft Word

Step 1: Open Microsoft Word

Click on the Microsoft Word icon on your desktop or search for it in your Windows search bar.

Step 2: Create a new document

Once you have opened Microsoft Word, select "Blank Document" from the menu or click on "New Document."

Step 3: Access the Header and Footer section

Click on the "Insert" tab in the toolbar. In the "Header & Footer" section, click on the "Header" or "Footer" button. A drop-down menu will appear with predefined options.

Step 4: Choose a header or footer template

Select a header or footer template from the drop-down menu, such as "Blank," "Simple," or "Elegant." Choose the one that best suits your document's style.

Step 5: Customize the header or footer

Once you have selected a header or footer template, you can customize it by adding text, inserting the date, inserting page numbers, and more. Click within the header or footer area to start editing.

Step 6: Insert page numbers

To insert page numbers, click on the "Page Number" button in the "Header & Footer" section. Select the desired location for the page numbers, such as "Top of Page" or "Bottom of Page." Choose a format for the page numbers from the available options.

Step 7: Customize page number format (optional)

If you want to customize the format of the page numbers, right-click on the inserted page number and select "Format Page Numbers." Adjust the settings as desired, such as starting page number, numbering style, and more.

Step 8: Save the document

Click on "File" and then "Save As" to save the document. Choose a file name and select the location where you want to save the file. Click on "Save."

Step 9: Close the document

Click on "File" and then "Close" to close the document.

Exercise:
Adding A Text Box In Microsoft Word

Step 1: Open Microsoft Word

Click on the Microsoft Word icon on your desktop or search for it in your Windows search bar.

Step 2: Create a new document

Once you have opened Microsoft Word, select "Blank Document" from the menu or click on "New Document."

Step 3: Position the cursor

Click on the location in the document where you want to insert the text box.

Step 4: Insert a text box

Click on the "Insert" tab in the toolbar. In the "Text" section, click on the "Text Box" button. A drop-down menu will appear with different text box options.

Step 5: Choose a text box style

Select a text box style from the drop-down menu, such as "Simple Text Box" or "Styled Text Box." Click on the desired style to insert a text box into the document.

Step 6: Enter text into the text box

With the text box selected, click inside it and start typing to enter your desired text. You can also copy and paste text from another source into the text box.

Step 7: Customize the text box

With the text box selected, you can customize its appearance using the options available in the "Format" tab in the toolbar. You can change the font, font size, alignment, fill color, and more.

Step 8: Resize and position the text box

Click and drag the corners of the text box to resize it, if needed. You can also click and drag the text box to reposition it within the document.

Step 9: Save the document

Click on "File" and then "Save As" to save the document. Choose a file name and select the location where you want to save the file. Click on "Save."

Step 10: Close the document

Click on "File" and then "Close" to close the document.

Exercise:
Adding Wordart In Microsoft Word

Step 1: Open Microsoft Word

Click on the Microsoft Word icon on your desktop or search for it in your Windows search bar.

Step 2: Create a new document

Once you have opened Microsoft Word, select "Blank Document" from the menu or click on "New Document."

Step 3: Position the cursor

Click on the location in the document where you want to insert the WordArt.

Step 4: Insert WordArt

Click on the "Insert" tab in the toolbar. In the "Text" section, click on the "WordArt" button. A drop-down menu will appear with various WordArt styles.

Step 5: Choose a WordArt style

Select a WordArt style from the drop-down menu by clicking on it. This will insert a default WordArt text box into the document.

Step 6: Enter text into the WordArt

With the WordArt selected, click inside the text box and start typing to enter your desired text. You can also copy and paste text from another source into the WordArt text box.

Step 7: Customize the WordArt

With the WordArt selected, you can customize its appearance using the options available in the "Format" tab in the toolbar. You can change the font, font size, fill color, outline color, and more.

Step 8: Resize and reposition the WordArt

Click and drag the corners of the WordArt text box to resize it, if needed. You can also click and drag the WordArt to reposition it within the document.

Step 9: Apply additional effects (optional)

To further enhance your WordArt, you can apply additional effects like shadows, reflections, and 3D effects. Explore the "Format" tab in the toolbar and experiment with different effects.

Step 10: Save the document

Click on "File" and then "Save As" to save the document. Choose a file name and select the location where you want to save the file. Click on "Save."

Step 11: Close the document

Click on "File" and then "Close" to close the document.

Exercise:
Adding A Watermark In Microsoft Word

Step 1: Open Microsoft Word

Click on the Microsoft Word icon on your desktop or search for it in your Windows search bar.

Step 2: Create a new document

Once you have opened Microsoft Word, select "Blank Document" from the menu or click on "New Document."

Step 3: Access the "Design" tab

Click on the "Design" tab in the toolbar. This tab contains options for customizing the document's appearance.

Step 4: Insert a watermark

In the "Page Background" section of the "Design" tab, click on the "Watermark" button. A drop-down menu will appear with predefined watermark options.

Step 5: Choose a watermark

Select a watermark from the drop-down menu, such as "Confidential," "Draft," or "Sample." The watermark will be inserted into the document.

Step 6: Customize the watermark

With the watermark selected, you can customize its appearance using the options available in the "Watermark" menu. You can change the font, size, color, and orientation of the watermark.

Step 7: Adjust watermark transparency (optional)

If you want to adjust the transparency of the watermark, right-click on the watermark and select "Format Watermark." In the "Format Watermark" dialog box, you can adjust the transparency slider to make the watermark more or less transparent.

Step 8: Save the document

Click on "File" and then "Save As" to save the document. Choose a file name and select the location where you want to save the file. Click on "Save."

Step 9: Close the document

Click on "File" and then "Close" to close the document.

Exercise:
Adding A Text Watermark In Microsoft Word

Step 1: Open Microsoft Word

Click on the Microsoft Word icon on your desktop or search for it in your Windows search bar.

Step 2: Create a new document

Once you have opened Microsoft Word, select "Blank Document" from the menu or click on "New Document."

Step 3: Access the "Design" tab

Click on the "Design" tab in the toolbar. This tab contains options for customizing the document's appearance.

Step 4: Insert a watermark

In the "Page Background" section of the "Design" tab, click on the "Watermark" button. A drop-down menu will appear with predefined watermark options.

Step 5: Select "Custom Watermark"

From the drop-down menu, select "Custom Watermark." This will open the "Printed Watermark" dialog box.

Step 6: Choose "Text watermark"

In the "Printed Watermark" dialog box, select the option for "Text watermark." This will allow you to create a custom text watermark.

Step 7: Enter watermark text

In the text box provided, enter the text that you want to use as the watermark. For example, you can enter "Confidential," "Draft," or any other desired text.

Step 8: Customize the watermark

You can customize the appearance of the watermark using the available options. You can choose the font, font size, color, layout, and orientation of the watermark.

Step 9: Adjust watermark transparency (optional)

If you want to adjust the transparency of the watermark, you can check the "Semi-transparent" option in the "Printed Watermark" dialog box. Use the slider to adjust the transparency level.

Step 10: Preview and apply the watermark

Click on the "Apply" or "OK" button to apply the watermark to the document. The text watermark will be added to the background of each page.

Step 11: Save the document

Click on "File" and then "Save As" to save the document. Choose a file name and select the location where you want to save the file. Click on "Save."

Step 12: Close the document

Click on "File" and then "Close" to close the document.

Exercise:
Adding A Picture Watermark In Microsoft Word

Step 1: Open Microsoft Word

Click on the Microsoft Word icon on your desktop or search for it in your Windows search bar.

Step 2: Create a new document

Once you have opened Microsoft Word, select "Blank Document" from the menu or click on "New Document."

Step 3: Access the "Design" tab

Click on the "Design" tab in the toolbar. This tab contains options for customizing the document's appearance.

Step 4: Insert a watermark

In the "Page Background" section of the "Design" tab, click on the "Watermark" button. A drop-down menu will appear with predefined watermark options.

Step 5: Select "Custom Watermark"

From the drop-down menu, select "Custom Watermark." This will open the "Printed Watermark" dialog box.

Step 6: Choose "Picture watermark"

In the "Printed Watermark" dialog box, select the option for "Picture watermark." This will allow you to add a custom picture as a watermark.

Step 7: Select a picture

Click on the "Select Picture" button to choose an image file from your computer. Navigate to the location where your desired picture is saved and click on "Insert" to add it.

Step 8: Customize the watermark appearance

You can customize the appearance of the watermark using the available options. You can choose the scale, washout, layout, and alignment of the picture watermark.

Step 9: Adjust watermark transparency (optional)

If you want to adjust the transparency of the watermark, you can check the "Semi-transparent" option in the "Printed Watermark" dialog box. Use the slider to adjust the transparency level.

Step 10: Preview and apply the watermark

Click on the "Apply" or "OK" button to apply the picture watermark to the document. The selected image will be added as the background watermark on each page.

Step 11: Save the document

Click on "File" and then "Save As" to save the document. Choose a file name and select the location where you want to save the file. Click on "Save."

Step 12: Close the document

Click on "File" and then "Close" to close the document.

Exercise:
Changing Page Color And Adding A Page Border In Microsoft Word

Step 1: Open Microsoft Word

Click on the Microsoft Word icon on your desktop or search for it in your Windows search bar.

Step 2: Create a new document

Once you have opened Microsoft Word, select "Blank Document" from the menu or click on "New Document."

Step 3: Access the "Design" tab

Click on the "Design" tab in the toolbar. This tab contains options for customizing the document's appearance.

Step 4: Change page color

In the "Page Background" section of the "Design" tab, click on the "Page Color" button. A drop-down menu will appear with a variety of color options.

Step 5: Select a page color

Choose a page color from the drop-down menu by clicking on it. The selected color will be applied to the entire page.

Step 6: Add a page border

Still on the "Design" tab, click on the "Page Borders" button. This will open the "Borders and Shading" dialog box.

Step 7: Choose a border style

In the "Borders and Shading" dialog box, select the "Page Border" tab. Choose a border style from the options available, such as a solid line, dashed line, or double line.

Step 8: Customize the border

Use the options in the "Settings" section to customize the border further. You can adjust the color, width, and style of the border.

Step 9: Apply the page border

Once you have customized the border, click on the "OK" button to apply it to the page.

Step 10: Save the document

Click on "File" and then "Save As" to save the document. Choose a file name and select the location where you want to save the file. Click on "Save."

Step 11: Close the document

Click on "File" and then "Close" to close the document.

Exercise:
Changing Page Layout In Microsoft Word

Step 1: Open Microsoft Word

Click on the Microsoft Word icon on your desktop or search for it in your Windows search bar.

Step 2: Create a new document

Once you have opened Microsoft Word, select "Blank Document" from the menu or click on "New Document."

Step 3: Access the "Layout" tab

Click on the "Layout" tab in the toolbar. This tab contains options for customizing the page layout of your document.

Step 4: Adjust page margins

In the "Page Setup" section of the "Layout" tab, click on the "Margins" button. A drop-down menu will appear with predefined margin options.

Step 5: Choose a margin setting

Select a margin setting from the drop-down menu by clicking on it. The selected margin setting will be applied to the entire document.

Step 6: Change page orientation

In the "Page Setup" section, click on the "Orientation" button. Choose either "Portrait" or "Landscape" from the drop-down menu. This will change the page orientation for the entire document.

Step 7: Set page size

Still in the "Page Setup" section, click on the "Size" button. Choose a page size from the options provided, such as Letter, A4, or Legal. The selected page size will be applied to the document.

Step 8: Customize columns (optional)

If you want to divide your document into multiple columns, click on the "Columns" button in the "Page Setup" section. Select the desired number of columns from the options available.

Step 9: Apply a page break (optional)

If you want to start a new page at a specific location in your document, place the cursor at the desired position and click on the "Breaks" button in the "Page Setup" section. Choose "Page" from the drop-down menu. This will insert a page break.

Step 10: Save the document

Click on "File" and then "Save As" to save the document. Choose a file name and select the location where you want to save the file. Click on "Save."

Step 11: Close the document

Click on "File" and then "Close" to close the document.

Test 1

Instructions:

Complete the following tasks using Microsoft Word. Remember to save your document upon completion.

Task 1: Opening Microsoft Word (2 points)

1. Open Microsoft Word from your computer's applications menu.

Task 2: Creating a New Document (3 points)

1. Create a new blank document.

2. Type the title "My First Document" at the top of the page.

3. Center-align the title text.

Task 3: Formatting Text (4 points)

1. Format the title text with **Georgia f**ont style, size 18, and make the color red.

2. Below the title, type a paragraph of text.

3. Apply bold formatting to the first sentence of the paragraph.

4. Change the alignment of the paragraph to justify.

Task 4: Inserting a Picture (3 points)

1. Insert a picture of your choice into the document.

2. Resize the picture to fit within the document width.

3. Position the picture below the paragraph of text.

Task 5: Adding a Bulleted List (3 points)

1. Create a bulleted list with at least five items related to your document topic.

2. Ensure the list is properly formatted with bullets.

3. Place the bulleted list below the picture.

Task 6: Saving the Document (2 points)

1. Save the document to your computer.

2. Choose a suitable file name for the document.

Task 7: Closing Microsoft Word (1 point)

1. Close Microsoft Word application.

Scoring:

- ❖ Each task is worth the indicated number of points.
- ❖ For each task, full points will be awarded if the task is completed correctly and partially if there are minor errors.
- ❖ The maximum achievable score is 18 points.

Test 2

Duration: 60 minutes

Instructions:
1. This practical test is designed to assess your proficiency in using Microsoft Word.
2. You will be presented with a series of tasks that you need to complete using Microsoft Word.
3. Read each task carefully and perform the required actions to complete the task.
4. Complete the tasks in the given order.
5. You can refer to any available resources or use the software's features and functions to complete the tasks.
6. Once you have finished the test, review your work for any errors or omissions before submitting it.
7. Submit your completed test within the given time limit.

Task 1: Formatting Text (10 points)

Format the following paragraph using the given specifications:

"The quick brown fox jumps over the lazy dog.

The quick brown fox jumps over the lazy dog.

The quick brown fox jumps over the lazy dog.

The quick brown fox jumps over the lazy dog."

a) Apply bold formatting to the first sentence.
b) Underline the second sentence.
c) Apply italics to the third sentence.
d) Change the case of the fourth sentence to uppercase.

Task 2: Creating a Bulleted List (10 points)

Create a bulleted list with the following items:

- Apples
- Bananas
- Oranges
- Grapes

Task 3: Inserting and Formatting a Table (15 points)

Create a table with 3 columns and 4 rows. Populate the table with the following data:

In the first column: Name, Age, Occupation

In the second column: John, 25, Engineer

In the third column: Lisa, 30, Teacher

Apply a table style of your choice to the table.

Task 4: Inserting and Formatting an Image (15 points)

Insert an image of your choice into the document. Resize the image and position it to the right side of the page.

Task 5: Creating a Header and Footer (10 points)

Create a header that includes your name and the document title. Create a footer that includes the page number on the right side.

Task 6: Applying Page Borders and Page Color (10 points)

Apply a page border of your choice to the document. Set the border width to 3 points. Change the page color to light blue.

Task 7: Using Find and Replace (10 points)

Find and replace all instances of the word "Lorem" with "Ipsum" in the document.

Task 8: Recording and Running a Macro (10 points)

Record a macro that performs any formatting action of your choice. Run the macro to apply the formatting to a selected paragraph.

Task 9: Adding a Text Box (10 points)

Insert a text box anywhere in the document and type the text "This is a text box". Format the text box with a border and fill color of your choice.

Task 10: Saving and Submitting the Document (10 points)

Save the document with the file name "Word_Practical_Test". Review your work and ensure all tasks are completed accurately. Submit the saved document to the test administrator.

Note: Each task carries a specified number of points, totaling 100 points. Make sure to complete all tasks within the given time limit. Good luck!

Test 3

Instructions:

Complete the following tasks using Microsoft Word. Follow each step carefully and save your document upon completion. Each task carries a certain number of points. Points will be awarded based on the accuracy and completeness of each task.

Task 1: Opening Microsoft Word and Creating a New Document (5 points)

1. Locate and open Microsoft Word on your computer.

2. Create a new blank document.

Task 2: Typing Text (10 points)

1. Type the following text into your document:

The quick brown fox jumps over the lazy dog.

2. Italicize the text.

Task 3: Formatting Text (10 points)

1. Underline the phrase "The quick brown fox."

2. Bold the word "lazy".

3. Change the font color of the word "dog" to red.

4. Apply strikethrough formatting to the word "jumps".

5. Change the font size of the entire sentence to 14.

Task 4: Adding a Table (10 points)

1. Insert a table with 3 rows and 3 columns.

2. Merge the cells in the first row to create a single cell.

3. Enter the numbers 1, 2, and 3 into the cells of the second row.

4. Enter the words "A", "B", and "C" into the cells of the third row.

Task 5: Inserting a Picture (10 points)

1. Insert any picture of your choice from your computer into the document.

2. Resize the picture to fit within the width of the document.

Task 6: Saving the Document (5 points)

1. Save your document to the Desktop.

2. Name the document "Microsoft_Word_Exam".

Task 7: Final Review (5 points)

1. Proofread your document for any spelling or grammatical errors.

2. Correct any errors found.

Task 8: Submitting Your Exam (5 points)

1. Save your work again to ensure all changes are saved.

2. Close Microsoft Word.

3. Insert the image at the beginning of the document.

4. Resize the image to a width of 200 pixels.

Task 4: Page Numbers

1. Insert page numbers at the bottom of the document, aligned to the center.

2. Start page numbering from the second page.

Task 5: Spell Check

1. Run a spell check on the entire document and correct any identified errors.

Submission:

1. Save the document with the file name "YourName_WordTest_Date.docx".

2. Submit the saved document to

Dear Readers,

In conclusion, "Word Mastery : Step By Step Exercises & Tasks" has been a labor of love for me as an author. I am thrilled to have had the opportunity to guide you through the vast potential of Microsoft Word and help you tap into your creative genius. Throughout this journey, we have explored the intricacies of document formatting, graphic design, and the art of captivating visual presentations.

I sincerely hope that this book has provided you with valuable insights, practical skills, and the confidence to transform your ideas into stunning creations. Remember, Microsoft Word is not just a word processing tool; it is a gateway to limitless possibilities for expression and communication.

But this is just the beginning of our adventure together. I am excited to announce that this book is the first installment in an upcoming series that will delve even deeper into the world of digital creativity and productivity. In the forthcoming volumes, we will explore advanced techniques, uncover hidden features, and unlock the full potential of Microsoft Word.

I am grateful for your trust in me as your guide and encourage you to continue honing your skills, experimenting with new ideas, and pushing the boundaries of what is possible. Your journey towards becoming a master of Word and a trailblazer in the digital landscape is only just beginning.

Thank you for joining me on this incredible journey, and I look forward to embarking on the next chapter together.

Yours creatively,

Rahim Deeds

Author of "Word Mastery : Step By Step Exercises & Tasks"